KALA'S KUNG FU

THE MOST ADVANCED MARTIAL ARTIST NEVER KNOWN

[1st In the Series of "Subtle and Metaphysical Martial Arts Made Simple"]

Rudra Natyananda

All rights reserved 2025 Adam Gonzales
BrainBlynd Publishing

No part of this book may be reproduced, or stored in a retrieval system, or transmitted in any form or by any means, electronic, mechanical, photocopying, recording, or otherwise, without express written permission of the publisher.

Printed in the United States of America

INTRODUCTION

Kala is often misunderstood. To most, the name evokes a distant deity, cloaked in symbolism—dancing in fire, encircled by cosmic cycles, wielding weapons, draped in skulls. In modern perception, Kala is mythic, removed, *a figure of worship rather than study.* But to the trained eye—one that watches not only for movement but for the forces beneath movement—Kala is something far more intimate. Kala is a principle. A rhythm. A way of moving through this reality. And most importantly, Kala is a martial presence.

This book is not about worshiping Kala. It's about learning from Kala.

In martial arts circles, the East is often synonymous with China or Japan. People think of Shaolin monks, Okinawan katas, or the internal arts of tai chi. But few trace the roots of these expressions back to their more ancient source. Fewer still feel the pulse of Kala in those movements—the silent current flowing beneath thousands of years of martial discipline. Before there were belts, uniforms, or stylized forms, there was only rhythm. Before any named techniques, there was presence. And before there was war, there was dance.

Kala is not a god of destruction. Kala is time itself. The devourer and the revealer. Kala's movements are not about violence. Every gesture in Kala's kung fu reveals a deeper law: *what you can't flow with, you must learn to dissolve;* what you can't dissolve, you must learn to embody.

In this book we enter the subtle current of Kala's movement, not just as a metaphor but martial method.

Most martial arts focus on a specific form, punches, kicks. But Kala's Kung Fu begins where form ends. It begins with *what's barely visible:* the twitch before the leap, the pause before the strike, the breath before the breath. When learning Kala, we do not imitate; *we empty.* We empty until the rhythm enters us as a living force.

Kala's style is not patterned in the way most martial arts are. It doesn't care for fancy moves or linear attacks. It arises in spirals and disappears in stillness. *His "stances" are often transitions.* His "strikes" are often disruptions of rhythm. There is no master technique, only mastery of response. This is the first discipline of

Kala: *to listen so deeply to what is arising* that your movement becomes attuned to a micro-scale level of awareness.

To practice Kala is to enter an agreement with time. You do not fight it. You do not try to outrun it. You learn to feel it's breathing pulse. In martial terms, this becomes timing, distance, and rhythm. In energetic terms, this becomes presence, emptiness, and surge.

Modern martial arts tend to emphasize external outcomes. Punch harder. Kick faster. Grapple stronger. But Kala's kung fu trains a different body—one that moves from *subtle awareness rather than muscular power.*

This body is not visible in the mirror. It is the felt body. *The breath-body.* The energetic architecture that underlies each motion.

To approach Kala as a teacher is *to become aware of your own inner architecture*—not in abstract or mystical terms, but in practice. *Where is the weight? Where is the tension? What contracts when you focus? What releases when you let go?* **Kala teaches through contrast:** effort and effortlessness, tension and release, noise and silence. These are not just poetic ideas; ***they are training principles.***

The way you walk, the way you sit, the way you breathe—*these are your first lessons.* Because Kala does not appear in techniques. Kala appears in patterns. Patterns of reaction, avoidance, aggression, and surrender. Once these are seen clearly, martial movement becomes a mirror.

Many see martial arts as combative—something rooted in defense or domination. Kala dissolves that notion. To train in Kala's Kung Fu is not to train to fight others; it's to train so you can perceive forces—subtle and gross—and *learn to dance with them.* You're not opposing your opponent. You are learning to read them, feel their rhythm, and either **disappear or absorb.**

Imagine wind meeting a mountain. *Sometimes Kala is the wind,* slipping past you with no resistance. *Sometimes Kala is the mountain,* unmoving and still. *Sometimes Kala is the storm*—overwhelming, all-at-once, without any pause. These are not metaphors for states of mind. They are tactical options *embedded in energetic awareness.*

When we **stop viewing martial practice as violence,** we see it as *intelligence in motion.* Kala's style is active and reactive all at once. You move because you have already felt the trajectory—not just of an attack, but an intention, energy. It is listening—subtle sensitive listening to the different waves of motion and emotion that precede every moment.

To explore Kala's kung fu is also to return to martial arts' forgotten roots.

India, the land of yogic wisdom, is often seen as peaceful, spiritual, and still. But *stillness is not the absence of force*—it is in the very center of it. The oldest warrior traditions didn't separate physical movement from spiritual growth. The physical practice was the path. Breath, awareness, balance, and rhythm were not separate disciplines, all of it was integrated into one understanding.

We find evidence of these ancient principles encoded in temple carvings, mudras, and myths. But *they are not meant to be frozen in time.* Kala's dance—sometimes called tandava—is not a story. It is a living code, moving technology of destruction and creation. And for those who can see it, *it contains a full system of martial strategy:* root, rise, spiral, descend, dissolve.

China, Japan, and other lands gave their gifts to the martial world —but Kala reminds us that the root goes deeper. Not just geographically, but energetically. Before systems, there was only flow. Before rules, there was only rhythm, and before schools there was only presence.

Kala does not teach through linear progression, Kala teaches through immersion. Through watching what breaks your rhythm. Through noticing what you avoid. Through **understanding how energy moves when you stop trying to control it.**

In this practice, you may not sweat as much as in others—but *you'll feel more.* You'll become aware of the tension that hides within you. You'll see **how force arises before motion.** You'll begin to understand that martial movement at it's deepest, isn't about domination—*it's about freedom.*

And so the invitation is simple: *step into Kala's rhythm.* Let go of form as an idol, let go of the need to win or be perfect. Begin to move but *not from your muscles,* but from your deepest awareness. Feel the empty spaces in between actions. **Kala lives there.**

Kala's Kung Fu is not a style. It's a way of perceiving and participating in life's rhythms—*subtle, fierce, and eternal.* You are not learning to fight. **You are learning to feel.** To move in time with time itself....*Kala you are the Teacher! The Dancer!* **'The Dark One'**... **'The Clawed One'**... **'The Fanged One'**..

MAY THE ANCIENT MOVEMENTS OF KALA BE REVIVED!

-Rudra Natyananda

Kala's Kung Fu

We'll first begin with **Kala's subtle sword exercises.** This is the very moment you start to feel before you actually move. There's a moment of space that opens up when these moves are being performed. Subtlety and openness will be two core aspects through this whole practice of learning.

Hidden Element of Kala

Keep the hand open for Kala's sword. This is a hidden element of Kala.

This will also keep your blood vessels open. Just doing this one thing—*keeping your hands open and relaxed*—

Kala operates with relaxed energy that just seems chaotic.

Exercise 1

Re-enact as if you're **pulling a sword out from your waistband.** Imagine you have a sword there. Start with your left hand.

Steps

Step 1: Open and relax the left hand.

Step 2: Slowly move it to the right side of your hips —or quickly, as long as you have control.

Step 3: Grab the 'invisible' sword.

Step 4: Pull the sword out from the waist in a slow and controlled swipe to the left. This is the "initiation cut"

Step 5: Repeat on the opposite side

Invisible Sword Control

Now that you have this invisible sword, **you can control it.** You can move it around, **it becomes something real**—an invisible tool. This is how you can really gain some feeling for *Kala's energy.* You actually have to feel it, then you become it. Then you know it's real, you don't have to guess or wonder.

Exercise 2: Hold the Sword

Hold the sword out with a fully extended arm.

Steps

Step 1: Imagine holding your sword in front of you loosely.

Step 2: Hold one arm out fully extended while holding the sword.

Step 3: Move the sword from left to right.

Step 4: Move the sword up and down.

Step 5: Start to move the sword in circles—clockwise and counter-clockwise.

Practicing with a Sword

Now you can obviously practice all these exercises **with a real sword,** but I wouldn't recommend that. Start with an invisible sword and **then move to a stick**—yes, just a regular lightweight stick you find outside.

You'll start to get a feeling of swiftness once you get the hang of it. Remember to stay loose, to **let go of any tension.**
Then you can keep advancing from a simple stick to a plastic or wooden sword.

Energy Flow and Tantric Martial Arts

These exercises will start to build a **loose energy flow within you.** This is how you'll know if you're doing it correctly. A lot of these certain attributes have **never been addressed to Kala** or Kali. But this is actually at the heart of what you would call 'Tantric Martial Arts.' **Tantra is experiment,** direct knowledge. We are knowledge, so **we must learn ourselves.** Much has been forgotten!

Kala as a Flower

Kala is like a flower, he fully blooms. There is an Indian dance (Tandava) posture called **'Talapuṣpapuṭa.'** This is a special posture.

It fully opens the body in a very subtle way. In English it means *'Flower-handful,'* and the posture shows that very act of holding out flowers as an offering. The offering is also the load before the strike itself. The empty moment, it's very subtle…

Ancient Postures

These postures are ancient, not very popular in the West yet. But in India they do connect like a wide net, **going back in time.** You can directly see these subtle postures and movements within almost **all of the Indian 'gods.'** It still hasn't been fully understood how large and ancient the Indian culture and pantheon of deities actually are.

Circles from the Heart

At the heart of this, **Kala is creating circles.** These circular movements come from the heart. He is moving in a multi-dimensional realm of **absolute grace and symmetry.**

Related to Kala, the Kalachakra is an older form of Kala. These forms or 'deities' have not been directly connected together yet in martial philosophy, but they are all connected.

Exercise 3: Throw the Sword Like a Baseball

Steps

Step 1: Hold your invisible sword at your left side. Make sure your left fist is out in front of you. Look ahead.

Step 2: Pick up your sword as if you were getting ready to throw a baseball.

Step 3: Now swing it to your opposite side behind you, as if you were throwing a baseball to someone behind you. Remember to keep the feet wide while you do it.

Balance and Precision

It's very important you stay **balanced on your feet while you do all this.** If you are not, then you aren't doing it like Kala. Everything Kala does is timed and of precision. **Swiftness comes with practice,** and eventually everything should be swift and easy. Until you get used to this, you won't be able to go into the higher 'chaotic' states. **First master the calm.**

You should be in control of your root (pelvis) while doing all this. Everything should be aligned and intact within your body.

General Rule in Practice

As a kind of general rule when practicing Kala's Kung Fu, you always want to **keep one foot in front of you.** You'll understand why later on. Right now, it's more about feeling and less about mentally grasping.

BECOME KALA. Don't think about him. Don't 'think' about his moves.

Purpose of the Exercise

This is the greater purpose to these exercises—you want to **fully feel the energy of Kala,** and the directions he moves in.

Exercise 4: Pulling the Sword Out from Behind You

Steps

Step 1: Raise your hand up to above your shoulder level.

Step 2: Grab your 'sword.'

Step 3: Imagine as if pulling it out from behind you.

Step 4: Let the arms rest to the sides.

Benefits of the Exercise

This exercise will loosen the back and shoulders **when done properly.** You should feel **deep muscles stretch in your upper back.** Every movement will flow together once you properly understand the dynamics and proper mechanics of Kala.

KALA IS NOT JUST A SYMBOL. KALA IS A FORCE.

The Aspect of Rolling within Kala

Kala will **roll everything at the same time**—his head will move right, eyeballs go left, left foot will step out for a wide stance. This aspect of rolling in Kala **has a lot to do with your muscles and bones shifting** in micro-movements. With so many muscles in the body, especially the ones around your spine, you can subtly shift and release layers. This opens the body up for more movement.

 Once you unlock these certain body patterns, then you can start to move with tremendous energy—or what you can call 'chaotic energy.'

FIRST KALA IS CALM

The Storm Before Movement

Just like before a powerful storm comes… **everything slows down, it gets dark.** Before the thunder and high winds, there is a **moment of cool calmness.** This is Kala—he is in control of what he's doing.

His nature is triumphant. KALA IS NOT A KILLER. HE IS A CLEANER.

Kala as the Monkey Woman King

This might sound strange at first, but Kala can be considered *the 'Monkey Woman King.'* I have been using 'he' to describe Kala so far, **but wide and spacious movements can be considered 'female.'** Since ancient times in religion and symbolism, anything very wide and round meant it was female. So don't overthink it—just understand the symbolism.

Kala's wide and circular nature can have that symbolism. **Every chop, every hack or rip—that vicious energy** *(you might only think of it as vicious)* **can actually be considered female.** *Because female nature is related with elegance, you do have to be elegant to do this.*

KALA IS COMPLETELY AGILE like a monkey…

Kala as Monkey

This is why I say Kala is also like the monkey. **He's mastered being soft and agile.** Remember to keep your knees soft for proper grounding. A lot of things are very subtle. Even though it seems simple, and is...there's a lot of little things to remember, they'll all integrate for a **full and complete system**—a 'model,' you can say.

One of the Oldest Models

But I say this is one of the oldest models, possibly ***the original for Kung Fu itself.*** *It's just not recognized or addressed.*

KALA... Kung Fu ORIGINATOR WILL RETURN...

Kala Kicks!

The Importance of Kicking in Kala's Kung Fu

In this section we'll be talking about the importance of kicking in Kala's Kung Fu. You first have to start **practicing to stand on one foot.** This seems mundane and really it is, but you'll understand why it's needed later.

Balance is key—remember, by just standing on one leg, **you are building a solid base.** You can easily learn to balance this way. A lot of people think about this stuff but never try.

Exercise 5: Standing on One Leg While Staying Aware

Steps

Step 1: Pick up your left leg calmly.

Step 2: Hold it either in front of you or behind you, or alternate between the two. This builds rhythm and balance. Start at your own pace and work your way up. The main thing you need while doing this is your balance. That's the whole purpose of this exercise.

The key is relaxed balance

Remember to Keep Blood Flowing Through Your Feet!!

The Active Force

The main component of Kala's movements are initiated ***through the legs and inner thigh muscles.*** There is a certain way of moving to where ***every movement will open up the hips*** and allow the whole body to open.

You have to keep the upper body free. In order to do that, you have to know how to free the lower body first.

You're fully expanding—remember, keep that in mind through this practice. Don't forget that.

Developing a Grounded and Stable Gait

The next movement will develop a grounded and stable gait.

Exercise 6: Standing with Legs Wide While Hands Are Crossed

Steps

Step 1: Widen your legs and stand in a lightweight manner. Your legs should take the shape of a triangle. *Only do what's comfortable.*

Step 2: Cross your right hand over your left hand around the waist area.

Step 3: Look straight ahead with your head slightly up.

Step 4: Feel your gait. Your base of the spine should be comfortable; your whole body should be.

Step 5: Slightly lean back.

Benefits of the Exercise

This exercise will create **a natural wide base and a natural expansion.** In a modern way of thinking, this exercise is like the action you take before swinging a baseball bat.

Developing Grounded and Swift Force

You need to develop force, **but grounded force with no breaks.** When I say breaks, **I mean imbalances.** Imbalances in the body **are moments of non-rhythm.** In Kala, there is always rhythm. There may be a pause, **but not a break.**

General Rule of Kala's Kung Fu

Never break or pop your bones!

Warning

This is something not usually talked about in the West. But **why is everybody popping and cracking their bones?** PLEASE DON'T DO THIS. *This will ultimately destroy any flow you have.* You never want to hear cracks in your bones. **Never.**

KALA IS FULL OF AIR. HE IS FULL. HE IS EMPTY. NOTHING IN BETWEEN.

Building Your Base

You have to build your base. **This base is the hollow and full point**—the point of all movement and non-movement. **In Kala, it's always there.** He never loses his base or balance.

Remember that some things are very simple but still subtle. **Kala's Kung Fu has a lot of secret aspects.**

The Purpose of Simple Actions

You twist, you turn, you chop—***simple actions.*** But are you doing them right? That's the purpose of this book: to show how very simple actions and movements come from an ancient source.

Declaration
KALA WILL BE REVIVED

Control and Balance

Kala has control over his lower legs, below his knees. *He has full control in that area.* This is how he keeps his balance so well.
ALWAYS KEEP THIS IN MIND

Movement and Striking

Kala can step forward, move back, and stand still **all at once.** Every strike **comes from the base.** Kala doesn't punch with his arms. He punches and strikes with his base. **The base becomes the entire body**—like an egg.

Exercise 7: Kala Foot Shifts

Steps

Step 1: Stand in a relaxed pose, feet slightly wide out like a duck.

Step 2: Shift your left foot up and to the left, get ready to step forward.

Step 3: Step forward with your right foot.

Step 4: Land on your right foot, but land on your base—your full body. Pause and make sure your erect and properly aligned. This is about full body control, alignment, and relaxation.

Step 5: Take another step. Feel that your energy is light and transferable. Continue to step 3-4 steps forward in a line, and then turn and reverse your direction. Build a rhythm once you get comfortable.

Benefits:

This will naturally start to build a grounded feel within you, it will also strengthen your control when stepping and turning. After some time you'll be much quicker when stepping.

The ankles have to be gently agile through all of this.

Kala's Nature

KALA IS FIERCE

KALA IS AGILE

So you should be *fierce and agile at the same time.*

Levels of Kala's Practice

Kala works on different levels:

1. The upper body sphere
2. The middle body sphere
3. The lower body sphere

Motion and the Matrix

Throughout this manual we'll be going through the motions of these spheres. Each sphere has a certain range of motions, almost all curved and circular motions: *twists, bends, turns, steps, grabs, letting go.*

These are all part of Kala's matrix. One of the keys to understanding this style is **grasping the overall nature** before you start individual moves.

Looking Up

Remember to **look up while doing these moves.** Kala almost always has his head up, ***roaring like a lion.*** He does this at different angles while he moves.

Kala always has control over his pelvic base. This pelvic base is like a control center, a command center. It's always intact, no matter how rapid and chaotic the movements are. At the same time, he can easily stand on his toes because every limb in his body is 'unlocked'.

Freedom

KALA IS FREE
This is why **he 'seems' so 'destructive.'** Most of these concepts can actually be applied. That's the beauty of it.

Kala's Swiping Motions

Kala has a certain **swiping motion when he moves. All of his moves are somewhat swiping in nature.** You can practice this by first softening the fingers. Always keep the fingers soft.

Unlocking

KEEP REMEMBERING THAT KALA IS FULLY UNHOOKED OR UNLOCKED.

This is why he is able to expand and contract so easily.

The Bull

Kala's force is unstoppable, like a bull moving forward.

KALA IS THE BULL

Fighting from Emptiness

Kala fights from an empty space inside him. Remember the subtleness.

It's a hollow and empty space, like the shape of a seed. It's within all of us.

Nature and Power

I believe this nature is in everything—creatures, planets, plants, and flowers. **We're born with a certain power.** It seems like all living things are born with power.
In Egyptian days there was the word NETER, like 'nature.' NETER was like God—pure power. There was also the word NETERU, which was the 'nature-beings' or 'God-beings,' beings with power.
This 'power' could really be a simple thing.

From a western point of view it can seem or sound bland. But from an eastern point of view it's everything —*movement, mind, air,* were all synonymous.

Power in All Creatures

So a bird—even just a small little bird—has so much power! We seem to kind of overlook these things. Every living thing has so much power. Just the power to be able to move in mysterious ways.

Study the movements of the leopard. In ancient times, animals were real power symbols. Today it's almost turned into mere cartoon or primitive. But these held a lot of power. It was almost like an oath to your spirit, your 'animal spirit.'

Spirit and Movement

THE ANIMAL IS SPIRIT
SPIRIT IS MOVEMENT
STUDY THE MOVEMENTS
DON'T FORGET THE RHYTHMS

We are part of that rhythm. It's a constant rhythm.

THIS IS KALA

Exercise 8: The Bull Walk

Steps

Step 1: Take 3 steps forward with your head slightlu swaying from left to right, but balanced.

Step 2: Turn your body around in the manner of a bull to take 3 steps forward from where you started.

Step 3: Continue to build up a momentum. This will be the base exercise before adding extra qualities to the walk. Eventually it will become 'Kala's Walk.'

Planes and Movement

In practice, you should move between 2 planes: **one horizontal and one vertical.** These planes wobble like the earth does on its axis.
These planes and wobbling factor will have a lot to do with how relaxed you are.

Staying wide in the body is necessary. Kala's waist is level and center, then it starts to tilt and move.

Arteries Open

All of Kala's major arteries are open—*the ones in his feet, the ones in his stomach. There is a major artery that runs through these areas.*

Muscles Relaxed

You have to relax **the intercostal muscles,** especially the inner thigh muscles connected to your hamstrings. All those muscles must be relaxed *so they can properly stretch.*

This is what allows your body to open like it does in Kala's Kung Fu.

UNDERSTAND KALA TO BECOME KALA

Importance of the Pelvic Base

I must emphasize the importance of the pelvic base.

Control and Readiness

KALA ALWAYS HAS **CONTROL OVER HIS PELVIC BASE.** This in turn gives your legs full free accessible motion. Your legs are the initiators for movement, they are light and ready.

KALA HAS FULL CONTROL OVER HIS BODY.

Never Lose It

HE NEVER LOSES IT

Until a point... where Kala knows it's safe to let go. That's the strike, the slice, the hammer, the chop.

KALA'S ENERGY AND POSTURE

Kala is **always looking up.** It may seem like he's "possessed." In a way, he is... **he's completely absorbed with the energetic spirit** that is above him. He's always raised, erect... just like a python.

KALA IS FULLY ENERGIZED

But the spine has to be "raised." **You have to raise yourself up fully** to become like Kala. This is subtle but actually simple.

STAND LIKE KALA!

Raise your body to raise your energy.

Exercise 9: Kala's Eyeball Turns

Think of Kala as **moving gears.** Everything is **twisting and turning,** expanding from the inside out.

Step 1) Stand up erect with a level posture

Step 2) Slightly pick the head up, start to look to your left

Step 3) Turn your eyes to look all the way out of the corner of your left eye, hold it

Step 4) Slowly turn your eyes back to the center

Step 5) Repeat on the right side

Benefits:

Stretches **all the nerves connected to your eyes.** This will give you a clear mind, **necessary for chaotic movement.**

The Storm-Force of Kala

This practice will **also build more spatial awareness.** The wide-spaced postures will start to feel and become more natural. Overall, **this exercise will calm you.**

Calmness comes before chaos. The chaotic dance of Kala sits at the peak of his joy.

KALA IS CALM CHAOS

You can think of Kala as the 'Storm-Force' or 'Storm-Energy.' He travels the universe. Energy and power travel through Kala's body.

Power in Your Fingers

Kala **never loses the power in his fingers.** There is a subtle power there, **within your palms and your fingers.** But you have to first feel it **and then build on it.**

Don't be overwhelmed by the "upper winds" in the chest area. Remember, in ancient times the body was really seen as a universe within itself.

Keep your torso soft. You need soft hands and a soft torso.

Creating more Space

Don't only think of Kala's width *as horizontal or vertical,* think of it as Diagonal also. From one foot to the other, *you can create diagonal space* just by adjusting your stance. Creating diagonal space will also open up the nerves and **allow the muscles to fully expand.**

KALA HAS SIMPLE PRINCIPLES

First Understand them

See Kala, Watch Kala

Move like Kala.

IT IS AN INITIATION

YOU MUST SLOW DOWN

TO FULLY GRASP HIS NATURE

He's like a moving hologram, he won't slow down for you… but if you can grasp him, you can ride along with him.

Tarantula Movements

Hes like a standing Tarantula, every limb is agile and **ready for a bite.** Kala waits like a tarantula, for the perfect bite... **the Capture.**

Kala carries a noose. This noose is used for capturing actions, like joint locks, grabs & slaps.

All these moves are **due to his agile hands and limbs,** the fingers, everything is loose. Because of this looseness, Kala can easily twist and turn fluidly with ease. He holds his noose, ready for an easy capture, with one movement he can crush you.

Realistically all these movements are one, but they have to be **expressed in different ways.** This is why Kala has so many weapons, he goes in every direction.

*Reminder

The joints in the foot have to be **equally loose to the joints in your fingers.**

The softness within your joints **will convert to immense power.** This is actually where mudras come into play. Inter-locking your fingers
in different positions **will naturally soften the entire body.**

Once that happens,
your energy will naturally start to move from the center.

Remember that you must always **have a sense of control in your "gait."**

In physical terms it would be your pelvis or pelvic bowl. **This area is very sensitive and you should be careful** to not damage it.

Don't over-extend, over-reach, lean over or do anything imbalanced.

Your gait should ***always keep you level,*** even, sama (sama is even). ***Keep the gait soft and pliable.***

Even though Kala stands up straight and erect **he also leans.** This is one of his specialties.....the lean. He leans in **perfect counter-balances with his body,** in a way it is like he's drunk, he's only drunk from the energetic spirit! He easily leans and tips his body in different directions.

His quadriceps activate the leans... once you can relax and *let go of the quadricep muscles,* they will naturally allow *the body to drop into a sideward lean.*

You'll see Kala in these ecstatic leans, sometimes he might be holding a skull. These are actual instruments you can use or just visualize to strengthen the practice.

REMEMBER KALA IS SUBTLE
YOU MUST BE SUBTLE

You have to become the "Non-grasper"

You see, the reason Kala is able to grip his weapons so well is because **he doesn't hold on to things!** That's why he can move so well! It may not make sense at first, but **this is at the heart of Kala's Kung Fu,** you **HAVE TO LET GO OF THINGS.** Only then will you be able to obtain Kala's power.

KALA'S KUNG FU isn't just a "fighting style."

Every step & movement you make throughout the day should be like Kala, remember you aren't imitating Kala,

YOUR BECOMING KALA

TAKE SOFT STEPS,
Not heavy Stomps

Move smoothly like a Snake,
Kala is imbued with the Serpent Spirit.

His movements are Gliding in nature... he slithers.

I believe that the mechanics of Kala are ancient.
Look at postures of the mayans even, they are usually in ecstatic crouch like postures.

KALA IS UNIVERSAL

He is Universal movement, movement of the body with 0% stress...

You can say that he moves with "weightless energy"

Become weightless to shift all of your weight.

Everything must be open, like the gait. Not only do you need control over your gait but **you need the proper width,** so your able to take the long and wide steps Kala makes.

- Allow **the muscles in the stomach and waist to fully relax,** this is important. Remember **there are deep aortic veins that run through your stomach**, you don't want to put too much pressure there, keep the circulation flowing.

Don't think of circulation as some kind of psychological nuance, it is something you feel directly.

So before you train, understand and make sure there is ROOM for the energy to flow through you.

When I say everything in your body must release and
unlock, this is mainly if you are tense.
About 90% of us are tense, as adults with stressful lives, jobs, relationships, and living standards.
So it is understandable if you are.

When you release and unlock tensions, they may come from any part of the body.
But the main area you want to keep free and "unlocked" all the time are your feet.
All those little bones and muscles in your feet have to be free and loose, *no tension, no holding.*
Kala's mobility is impeccable, ***furiously storming with grace,*** KALA IS VERY MYSTERIOUS..

HE IS THE UNKNOWN SPACE

WRATHFUL GRACE

HE IS PLEASED TO CUT & RIP ANY ILLUSION
he's faced with

SECRET CONCEPTS OF KALA TO REMEMBER - FROM ORIGINAL SANSKRIT TERMS

-**Sammoha** - *"Fainting"*: Kala easily faints, this is because he doesn't hold on. With just one slip he can faint, and the faint turns into the strike.

-**Pralambita** - *"Suspended Down"*: Think of this like you are a puppet, you should let yourself "hang" from the energetic strings above.

-**Pravesa** - *"Entry/Entrance"*: This is where Kala will first begin, he enters with one large step. He crosses an invisible barrier before he starts, this creates the dimensional barriers! Do this before you start your practice, similar to a sumo wrestler before he begins.

-**Grathana** - *"Settling"*: Kala is fully settled in his body, this is why he's so stable. His core is like a seat, even while he's standing it's like he is sitting.

-**Prasrta** - *"Spreading":* Kala is spreading energy around, everything is widening, becoming spherical.

-**Drsti** - *"Vision/Glance/Peculiar Look":* Kala shows this in his ecstatic glances, it may seem odd. But this glancing is actually what widens his dance dimensions. And it soothes him, doing this actually soothes the whole body. Those nerve attachments in your eyes must relax.

-**Sphotana** - *"Bursting":* Kala bursts with almost every movement. With each step he takes he is ready to burst. The burst is a strike, every strike should be like a burst.

-**Valana** - *"Turning":* Another main aspect of Kala, he is always turning to counterbalance and gain momentum. The turn is an opening, a gateway of space being created before the strike.

-**Giti** - *"Rhythm":* There's always a rhythm being created, this will always apply in practice.

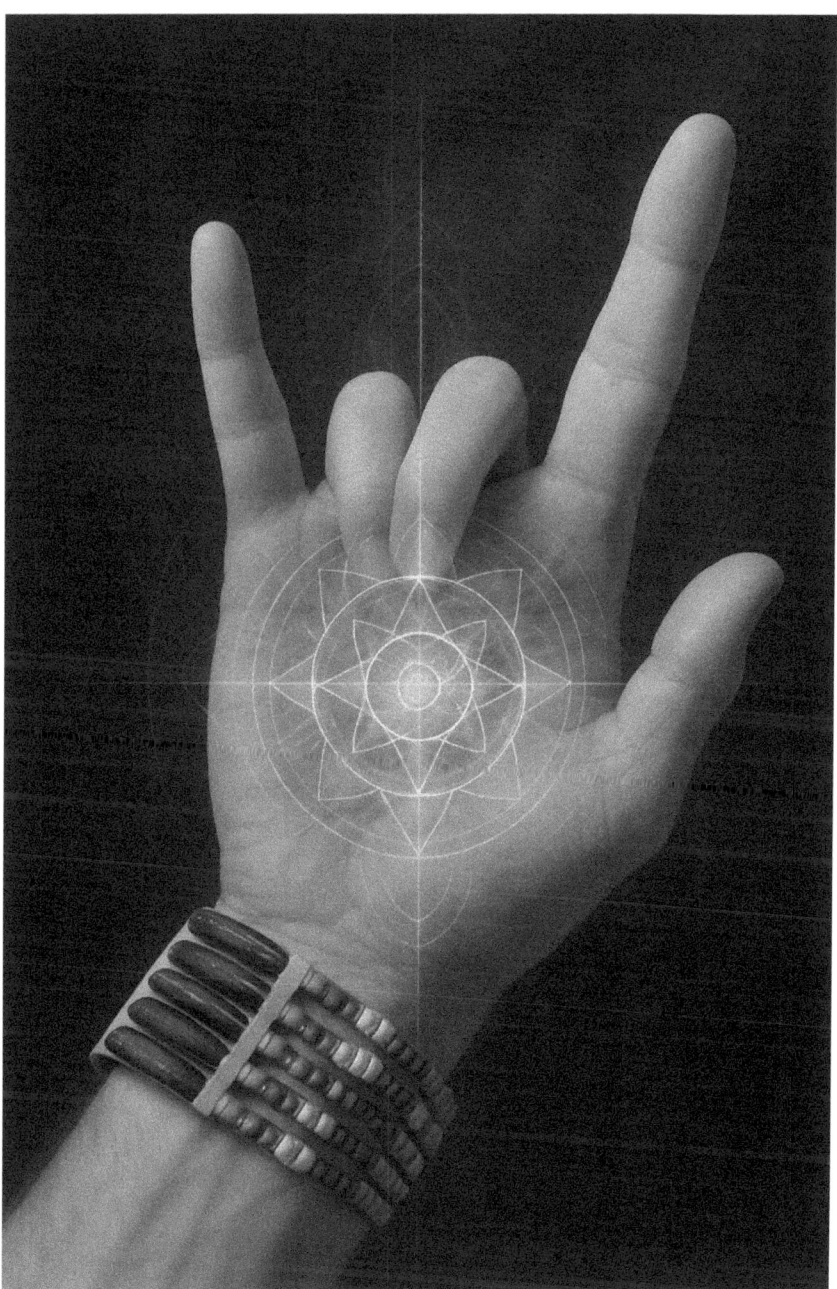

-Udvartana - *"Springing Up"*

When Kala fights or dances, he lightly springs up through his movements.
This light spring is also part of the reason he's so light on his feet.

-Lilangaharan - *"Sportive Limbs"*

Kala's limbs are acrobatic, loose but still in control, similar to a monkey.
Kala is the original sports player, all of his arm and hand positions are UNIVERSAL.
They can be seen in all sports like basketball, baseball, golf, tennis, volleyball, football...
ALL OF THESE ARE ACTIONS OF KALA!

-Vibhakta - *"Proper Proportion"*

All of your movements should be aligned in a way that energy flows. This is the purpose of keeping proper proportions.

-Ayatnaja Alamkara – *"Grace not forced"*

Never force anything within your body, posture, or any moves in general.
Forcing anything will tighten the body up and you'll be doing the exact opposite of what Kala is doing.

DON'T UNDERESTIMATE THE GRACE FACTOR

BEING GRACEFUL IS 90% OF THE TEACHING

3 FACTORS TO NEVER Forget while learning Kala's Kung Fu:

1) Be Centered

2) Be Upright

3) Be Graceful/Elegant/Yin

KALA IS ALWAYS LIGHT LIKE A LIZARD

HE IS COMPLETELY IN TUNE WITH REPTILLIAN LIKE MOVEMENTS

KALA LIVES IN YOUR LIMBIC SYSTEM, HE'S JUST ASLEEP...

DUE TO OVER-EATING, OVER-EXCITEMENT, STAGNATION, NON-CELIBACY, AND ANGER..

KALA IS NOT ANGRY!!

THIS GOES AGAINST BUDDHIST PRINCIPLES

KALA IS NOT ATTACHED

KALA IS NOT OBSESSED

AND KALA IS NOT MAD..

DON'T LET THE IMAGES CONFUSE YOU

KALA IS JUST IN TUNE WITH REALITY

HE DOESN'T THINK,

HE DOESN'T JUDGE,

HE JUST MOVES..

AND THERE IS NO STOPPING HIM

KALA IS THE KUNDALINI, THE RISING FORCE

HE'S LATENT WITHIN US…YOU MUST AWAKEN HIM TO TRULY UNDERSTAND

EVERY WEAPON KALA HOLDS, IS A REPRESENTATION OF AN ACTUAL FORCE WITHIN US

JOIN THE ORIGINAL SOURCE…THE ORGINAL FORCE…KALA!!

KALA HAS RETURNED

www.ingramcontent.com/pod-product-compliance
Ingram Content Group UK Ltd.
Pitfield, Milton Keynes, MK11 3LW, UK
UKHW020735050126
9886UKWH00069B/950